YOU AND YOUR CHILD
READING GAMES

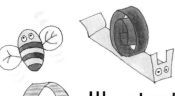

Ray Gibson

Illustrated by Simone Wood, Lucy Su
and Kim Blundell

Designed by Non Figg and Lindy Dark

Edited by Paula Borton

Series editors: Robyn Gee and Jenny Tyler

Photography by Ray Moller

Parents and children can have hours of fun playing games with words and letters, and this book provides lots of ideas to introduce your child to the pleasures of reading. All the projects encourage the development of basic reading skills, while building up a general awareness of written and spoken language in everyday situations.

First published in 1993 by Usborne Publishing Ltd, Usborne House, 83-85 Saffron Hill, London EC1N 8RT, England. Copyright © 1993 Usborne Publishing Ltd. The name Usborne and the device ⊕ are Trade Marks of Usborne Publishing Ltd.

Getting ready for reading

Games are a great way to help children become readers. They provide a relaxed and informal learning situation in which a child is actively involved. In playing a game a child can see a limited number of words or letters lots of times, but not in a boring or repetitive way.

The games in this book will help your child learn to recognize letters and whole words, to realize that speech sounds are represented by letters and to understand that words are made up of groups of letters. While helping make the things you need to play the games, your child will draw and paint letters and handle plastic magnetic alphabet shapes, so becoming familiar with the names of all the letters. Make sure that the letters you write are always in lower case, except for proper names. Once your child has grasped the alphabet names, you could gradually introduce the sounds each letter makes. Don't rush this as it is easy to get confused, particularly when some letters make a variety of sounds: "g" in giraffe and "g" in gate makes a totally different sound in each case.

Make sure your child enjoys playing the games. Only play when she wants to and give lots of praise and encouragement.

Reading skills

Learning to read is a complex process which involves bringing together a lot of different skills. The ability to talk and listen with attention, to absorb and understand information, to concentrate and to observe and interpret pictorial information all play an important part. Children also need to know and experience the world around them and realize that they must bring this knowledge into their reading to support their understanding and enrich their imagination.

Sharing books

Games can help in the development of reading skills, but the best and simplest way to help develop them is to share books with a child. Games can then be a valuable supplement by building upon and reinforcing your child's knowledge and confidence.

Looking at, discussing, reading and enjoying books is the single most important thing that parents can do to encourage their children to become readers. Apart from the skills it develops, learning that books can be a source of pleasure, entertainment and information gives children a strong incentive for learning to read.

A good way to introduce children to books is to talk about the pictures. Choose scenes, such as the one below, that tell a story and are full of detail and action; this prepares children for reading stories in words.

Reading aloud

Reading aloud to children helps to expand their vocabulary and comprehension and to improve their listening and concentration skills.

It is now known that children who find it hard to recognize which words rhyme with each other find it difficult to learn to read. This sheds new light on the importance of sharing rhymes and poems with young children.

Stories can be an immense source of pleasure to children, even before they fully understand them. They quickly develop enthusiasms for particular stories and will want well-loved books to be read over and over again. When the story becomes very familiar to a child she will often start to join in,

a b c d e f g h i j k l m

Picture sequences are ideal for showing children how a story works.

especially with catchy, rhythmical phrases. She may like to pretend she's reading, holding the book and relating the story in her own words. She may also enjoy putting in her own sound effects, for instance in an animal story.

Discuss the story with your child. Drawing pictures inspired by a story is one way for a child to express what he has understood. Ask him to tell you about his picture and what is happening in it, also what happened just before and will happen just after, so he can get a sense of the order of events.

Looking at pictures

Children who have plenty of opportunity to look at pictures and talk about them, learn to "read" the pictures to find out what is going on in them. This is very useful when they first start to read, as clues from the pictures give them confidence to try the words underneath. When you look at picture books together, ask your child questions about the pictures and discuss what is happening. Play "find" games. Ask her what happened just before the action in the picture and what she thinks will happen next.

Learning how books work

A child who is used to using and sharing books will already have absorbed a lot of information that is needed before learning to read. She will understand, for instance, that you start at the front and work to the back and that you tackle each page from top to bottom and from left to right. Allow her to turn the pages for you to reinforce the front to back movement. Using a finger to trace underneath the words as you read them will help develop the top to bottom and left to right movements of reading.

Making up stories

Make up stories to tell your child, or make them up together, perhaps by asking questions. These have the advantage of being tailor-made to suit your child's particular interests. This will help develop your child's sense of what a story is.

Words all around you

Once your child has learned to enjoy stories, rhymes, jokes, tongue twisters and so on, you can then help him develop a general awareness of the written word and its usefulness in all sorts of everyday situations in which you use reading and writing to gain and impart information.

Learning to recognize and even write his own name is an important step. It helps establish the idea that groups of letters say the same thing to everyone who reads them. Write messages and labels for your child. You could also make books together about things you both enjoy, reinforcing the idea that reading and writing are closely linked.

Playing games with letters and words can be an enjoyable part of the gradual process of learning to read. Games such as making bingo cards, fishing with magnetic letters and making an alphabet wall hanging bring together both writing and reading activities, and are a pleasurable way for your child to come to grips with the world of books and print.

n o p q r s t u v w x y z

Alphabet fishing game

You will need:
1 set of plastic magnetic letters in lower case
1 plastic straw for each player
strong thread
metal paper clips
rounded scissors
tape
ruler

To make the letter cards

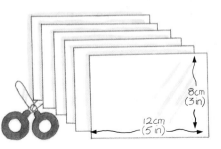

Cut strong white paper into six rectangles 12cm by 8cm (5in by 3in).

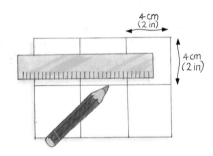

With a pencil, rule each piece into six squares.

Learning notes

This matching letters game will help your child become familiar with the names and shapes of the letters of the alphabet. Remember to say the letter names as they are fished.

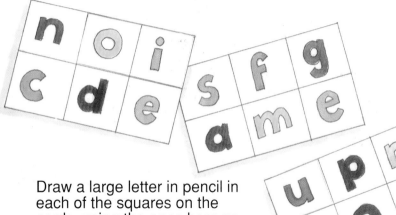

Draw a large letter in pencil in each of the squares on the cards, using the ones here as a guide. Then go over the letters in thick felt-tip pen.

To make the rods

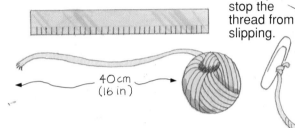

Add tape to stop the thread from slipping.

Cut a piece of thread about 40cm (16in) long for each of the straws.

Knot one end to a metal paper clip and wind the other end around the straw, and then tie a knot.

Hints

• Draw the letters roughly the same size as the magnetic ones to make the matching easier.

• Number each card on the back to make sure you get a different one each time you play.

thick felt-tip pens

pencil

strong white paper

To play the game

Each player has one card and a fishing rod. Spread out the magnetic letters, placing them upside down.

Each player takes turns fishing for a letter. Players try to match their fished letters to the letter shapes on their cards. If the letter matches, it is placed over the drawn shape, otherwise it is put back. The first player to fill her card with plastic letters wins the game. Once children have mastered this game, they can play with up to three cards at once.

Other ideas

Once your child is familiar with lower case, you could try this game using capital letters, or a mixture of the two.

If you can't find magnetic capital letters, make your own by cutting them out of paper and taping on a metal paper clip.

Place them face down. Use a magnetic letter tied to a straw as a "fishing rod".

Messages

Put short simple messages on the refrigerator door for your child to read, such as "look under the bed". Leave a small "prize" for your child to find.

5

The lazy zookeeper

One morning all the 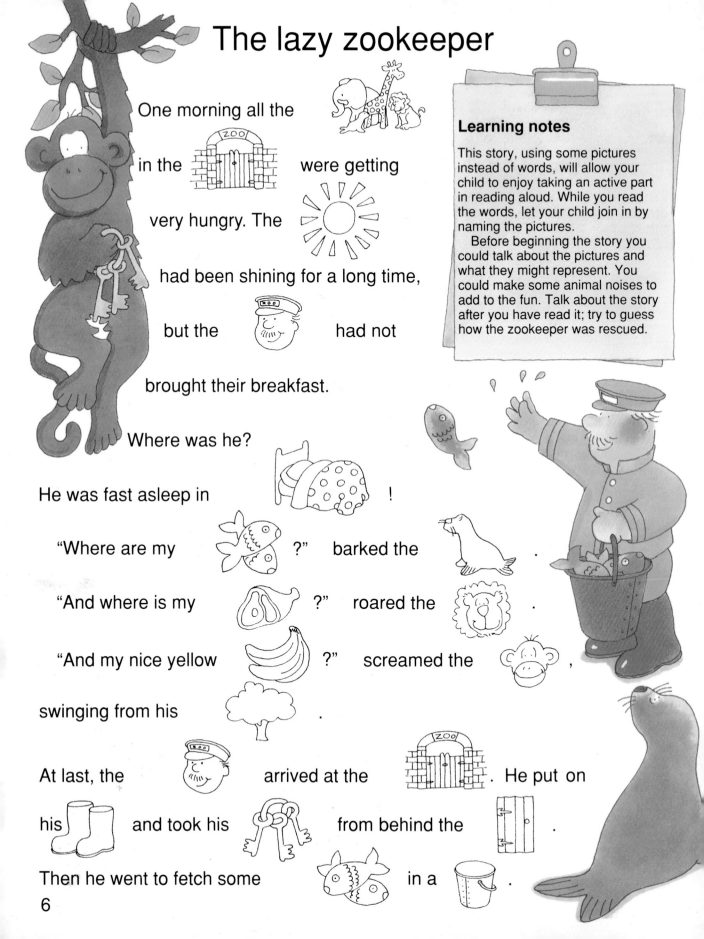 in the [ZOO] were getting very hungry. The [sun] had been shining for a long time, but the [zookeeper] had not brought their breakfast.

Where was he?

He was fast asleep in [bed]!

"Where are my [fish]?" barked the [seal].

"And where is my [meat]?" roared the [lion].

"And my nice yellow [bananas]?" screamed the [monkey], swinging from his [tree].

At last, the [zookeeper] arrived at the [ZOO]. He put on his [boots] and took his [keys] from behind the [door]. Then he went to fetch some [fish] in a [bucket].

6

Learning notes

This story, using some pictures instead of words, will allow your child to enjoy taking an active part in reading aloud. While you read the words, let your child join in by naming the pictures.

Before beginning the story you could talk about the pictures and what they might represent. You could make some animal noises to add to the fun. Talk about the story after you have read it; try to guess how the zookeeper was rescued.

Of all the  the was the hungriest and the

angriest - and the naughtiest! He stole the  from the

keeper's coat and ran off to let the out!

"Where is our breakfast?" they cried, chasing the around

and around. He ran into an empty  and banged the

 behind him. Only a little white felt sorry for

him, and crept in through the to keep him company

until help arrived.

"I will have three next to my bed from now on,"

said the , "so I will never be late again!"

And he never was.

Other ideas

Make your own picture poster together for your child's room. Use pictures cut from a magazine. It could say:

"This is my room. In it there is a and some I have some blue at my window..." and so on.

You could also try making up your own short story about a dog chasing a cat. Plan the story together. You could begin by asking such questions as "Where was the cat?" "What was she doing?"

Lily pond race

You will need: green paper, rounded scissors, large paper bag, black felt-tip pen

Learning notes

Coping with unfamiliar words can present problems, especially if they are not in context. Recognizing or "sounding out" the initial letter of a word can provide a powerful clue, and this game gives your child practice at this.

start

To make the frog

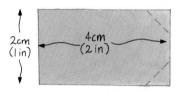

2cm (1in) 4cm (2in)

Cut a piece of green paper 4cm by 2cm (2in by 1in). Snip off the corners at one end.

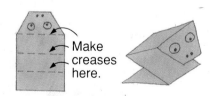

Make creases here.

Draw in the eyes and nose. Make three creases, as shown, then fold up the body so the frog sits up.

To make the caterpillar

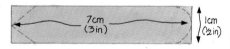

7cm (3in) 1cm (½in)

Cut another piece of green paper 7cm by 1cm (3in by ½in). Cut a pointed tail and a rounded head.

Fold the paper into a concertina shape. Make sure the tail lies flat. Draw in the eyes.

To make the cards

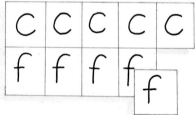

C C C C C
f f f f f

Cut thin white cardboard into ten squares 2cm by 2cm (1in by 1in). Write "c" for caterpillar on five squares and "f" for frog on the rest.

ruler

thin white
cardboard

To play the game

Put the cards in a paper bag
and shake it. Each player
takes turns to pick a card
and name the letter. If it is a
"c" the caterpillar moves one
place closer to the pond. The
frog moves if the letter "f" is
turned up. The first to reach
the lily pond is the winner.

Your child can also play
this game by herself as it is
the frog and caterpillar who
are racing each other.

Other ideas

You can make other paper
creatures to involve more
first letter sounds. Make
letter cards to match the first
letter.

S

Snail

Tape on a paper
"shell".

Moth

m

Cut the shape from
folded paper.

Worm

Curl up a strip of
paper and tape it at
the bottom. Draw in
its eyes.

b **Bee**

Draw and cut out a
paper bee.

9

Mice and cheese

You will need: pink paper, white paper, thin white cardboard, glue stick, ruler, pencil, tape, black felt-tip pen, scraps of paper or yarn, rounded scissors

To make each mouse

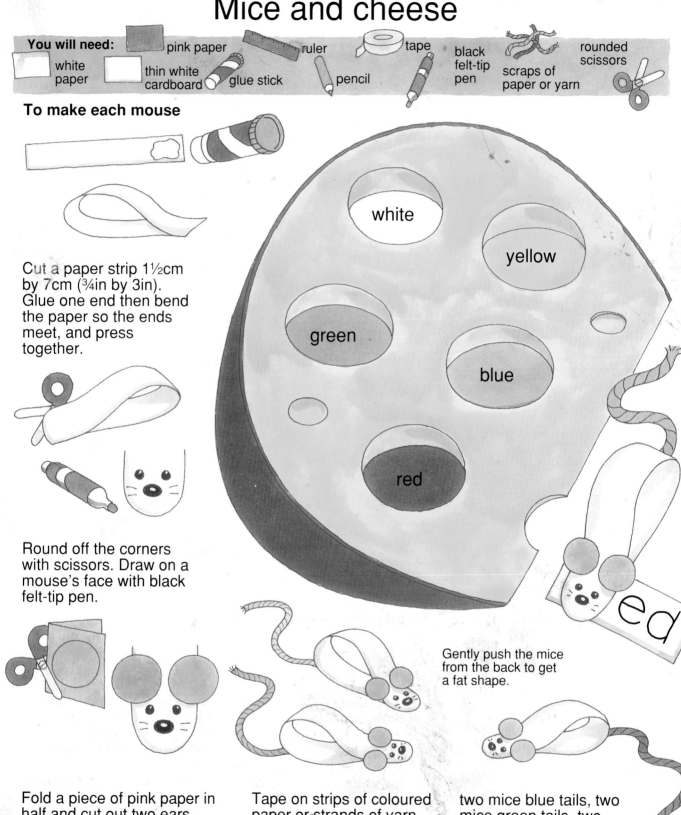

Cut a paper strip 1½cm by 7cm (¾in by 3in). Glue one end then bend the paper so the ends meet, and press together.

Round off the corners with scissors. Draw on a mouse's face with black felt-tip pen.

white

yellow

green

blue

red

ed

Gently push the mice from the back to get a fat shape.

Fold a piece of pink paper in half and cut out two ears. Glue them on so they stick up. Make ten mice altogether.

Tape on strips of coloured paper or strands of yarn for the tails, as shown. Give two mice red tails,

two mice blue tails, two mice green tails, two mice yellow tails and two mice white tails.

10

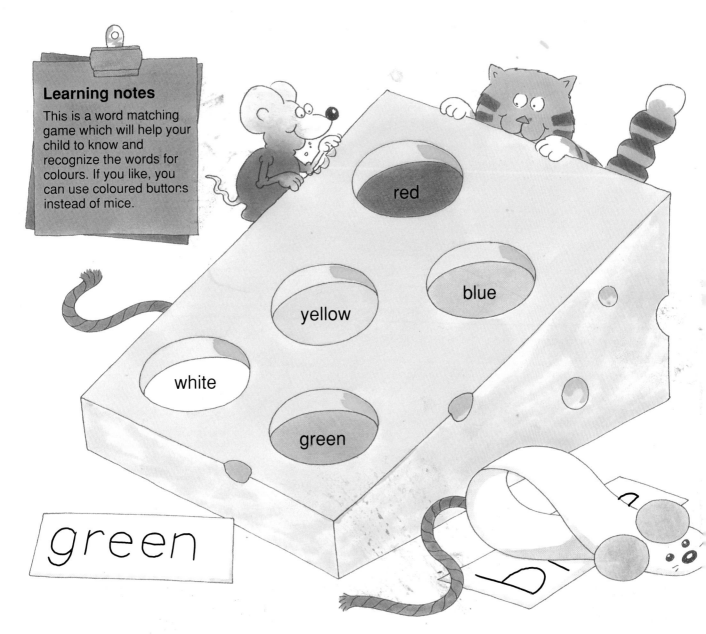

red

blue

yellow

white

green

green

To make the cards

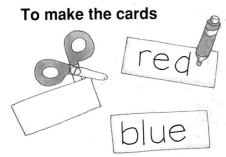

red

blue

Make ten cards 6cm by 3cm (2½in by 1½in). Write "red", "blue", "white", "yellow" and "green" on pairs of cards.

To play the game

This is a game for two. Divide the mice so that both players have five mice, one of each colour. The players each choose a cheese from this double page.

Spread the cards face down between the players who take turns picking up a card and reading the word. If the card, for example, says "red" the player can then put his red-tailed mouse on his cheese on the hole marked "red".

If the hole is already occupied, the card is put back. Move the cards around between turns. The first player to fill his own cheese wins.

Later on, you can cover the holes with paper circles marked with the names of other colours. Make mouse tails to match.

11

Time to go shopping

You will need: 1 set of plastic letters in lower case (you could use magnetic letters)   paper bag

Hints

•You could use plastic capital letters at a later stage.

•If you pull an "x" out of the bag, look for word endings, such as "box". If this is too difficult take the letter out of the bag.

To play the game

Put the letters in a bag. The players pick a letter and name it. They then see what they can "buy" with it by finding an object beginning with that letter. You could put counters on objects that have been bought.

12

Learning notes

This game will encourage your child to use first letters as clues to recognizing words. As you look at the picture, talk about the objects, allowing your child to identify by name as many as possible. If your child wants to name everything, you could start at the top left-hand shelf and work across, to encourage the usual left to right reading pattern.

Other ideas

Using the picture only
Try playing I-Spy. One player chooses the first letter of an object in the picture while others guess what it is.

Using the letters and objects in your room
Place the letters around the room. The players have to see if they have been put in the right place, for example, they take off the letter "c" from the table and place it on the chair. You could

put a time limit on this game to make it more exciting.

Using the picture and cards
On cards, write first and second letters of the objects which players have to guess, such as 'sn' for snake.

Spiders and drainpipes

You will need: 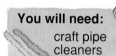 yarn 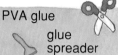 PVA glue rounded scissors 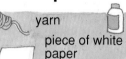 thick paper

craft pipe cleaners · piece of white paper · glue spreader · tape · black felt-tip pen

To make the spiders

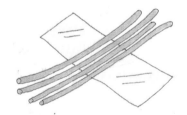

Cut a pipe cleaner in half and shape it into a ball. Tuck the sharp ends underneath.

Cut four pieces of yarn about 10cm (4in) long. Lay them close together on a strip of tape.

Press the ball firmly onto the tape so that it sticks. Now trim the tape on either side.

To make the cards

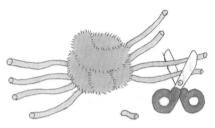

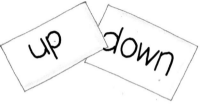

Trim the legs so they are even on both sides, about 3cm (1in) long.

Cut small eyes out of white paper. Glue them on and draw in the pupils with felt-tip pen. Make one spider for each player.

Cut 8 pieces of thick paper 4cm by 6cm (1½in by 2½in). Clearly write "up" on four of the pieces and "down" on each of the remaining cards.

Learning notes

This game will help your child learn to sight read simple words. Once "up" and "down" have become familiar you can introduce three "stop" cards to the pile. When a "stop" card is turned up, the spider must then stay where it is for that "turn". At a later stage you can make cards that read "go on one" and "go back one". This can be developed to "go on two", "go back two" and so on up to four. Remember to introduce only one number at a time.

Playing spiders and drainpipes

The object of this game is to see which spider can reach the web first.

Mix the "up" and "down" cards and place them in a pile in front of the players.

To start, place the spiders on the rain barrel at the bottom.

The first player throws the dice. The spider is then moved along the spaces according to the number shown on the dice. The next player has a turn and the game continues.

If a spider lands on the brick squares where two drainpipes meet, the player must pick up the top card on the pile and read the instruction. If it is an "up" card the spider must go up the drainpipe and if a "down" card is turned up, the spider is moved down. The card is then returned to the bottom of the pile.

To play the game you will need:

One spider for each player.

8 cards

dice

Hint

Instead of making "pipe cleaner" spiders, each player can draw a spider on a square of strong paper.

25

26

27

24

23

22

21

17

18

19

20

16

15

14

13

9

10

11

12

8

7

6

5

1

start

2

3

4

15

Bingo

You will need:
- stiff coloured paper
- stiff white paper
- thick black felt-tip pen
- paper bag
- rounded scissors
- 1 set of plastic letters

Cut stiff white paper into four rectangles 20cm by 10cm (8in by 4in). Draw eight squares onto each piece.

Cut out small pictures from magazines, not more than 5cm by 5cm (2in by 2in). Choose pictures so that you get a good mix of first letters.

Glue a picture onto each of the white spaces on the cards.

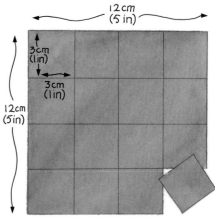

Put the cards aside to dry. In the meantime you can make the counters.

Cut a square of coloured paper 12cm by 12cm (5in by 5in). Then divide it into squares 3cm by 3cm (1in by 1in). Cut them out to make paper counters.

Hints

- If there are more than two players you will have to make more paper counters.

- You can be flexible when naming the pictures: "carrot" can also be "vegetable"; "rabbit" can also be "animal".

- Talk about the pictures as you cut and glue them. Emphasize the sound of the first letter as you say the words.

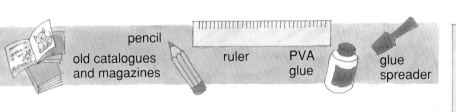

pencil

old catalogues
and magazines

ruler

PVA
glue

glue
spreader

To play the game

Put the plastic letters in a
paper bag. Remove any
extra letters so that you just
have the 26 letters of the
alphabet.

Each player has a white
picture card and eight paper
counters. Players take turns
pulling a plastic letter out of
the bag and saying its name.
Whoever has a picture
starting with that letter, places
a counter over that square

on his card. The letter is
then returned to the bag.
The first player to cover his
card is the winner. Swap the
cards around for each game.

Other ideas

Word bingo

At a later stage you can make
this into a word-reading game.
Make word cards to match the
pictures. Place them in a pile
face down and see if you can
match the words with the
pictures as they are turned over.
The cards are placed over the
pictures instead of counters.

Colour bingo

Play colour bingo by making cards with
only six spaces. Colour each square
differently. Write the names of the
colours on small squares
and put them in a bag.
Players play colour
bingo by matching the
words with the colours.

carrot

bee

house

hat

ring

red

ye

pink

green

blue

17

Country garden

You will need: thin white cardboard · coloured paper · rounded scissors · ruler · pencil · black felt-tip

ball

cake

gate

table

dog

flower

spade

bird

To make the cards and counters

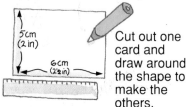

5cm (2in)

6cm (2½in)

Cut out one card and draw around the shape to make the others.

cake

tree

fish

Using a pencil and ruler, cut 20 cards measuring 6cm by 5cm (2½in by 2in) out of thin white cardboard.

On each of 16 cards write one of the words from the picture. On the remaining four cards draw a balloon. These four are your jokers.

Cut 16 counters about 2cm by 3cm (1in by 1½in) from coloured paper.

Learning notes

This word matching game is a fun way to help your child recognize simple words using pictures as clues. The game also encourages memory and concentration skills.

bee

tree

pig

fish

duck

horse

goat

cow

To play the game

This is a game for two players. Each player chooses one side of the double page - the field or the garden.

Lay the word cards in rows face down between the players. One person turns up a card and reads the word. If he can match that word to a word on his side of the page he leaves the card turned up and puts a counter over the word on the page. He turns the card back over if he cannot match the word. The other player then has a go and so on. If a joker card is turned up the player misses a go. Joker cards are left turned up. The first player to cover all the words on his side of the page is the winner.

Other ideas

Use the scene here as a "talkabout" picture or to play I-Spy . See if you can make up a story about the picture.

I can

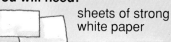

Learning notes

In this game, players are given plenty of practice in matching up identical words, using pictures to help. This will help your child start recognizing whole words without having to "sound out" each individual letter.

You will need:

 sheets of strong white paper

sheet of coloured paper

black felt-tip pen

I can

run

paint

eat

To make the word cards and paper counters

Cut some strong white paper to make 30 cards about 8cm by 4cm (3in by 2in) each.

dance

swim

cook

With a pencil, clearly write all the words from this double page onto the cards, one word per card. Then go over the letters in black.

blow

talk

drink

Now cut 30 squares from coloured paper about 2cm by 2cm (1in by 1in). These are your counters.

count

wash

drive

pencil

ruler

rounded scissors

Hint
Use an envelope to store the words and counters.

fly

kick

cry

read

skate

jump

smell

sleep

brush

hide

stretch

dig

To play the game

This is a game for two.

One player decides to be Mouse, and the other player is Cat. Now divide the word cards into two piles, face down, one for Cat and one for Mouse.

The first player then turns over a card from her pile saying "I CAN" and tries reading the word. She can use the pictures and words on the page to help. Whoever has that word on his or her side of the page then covers that word with a paper counter.

The second player now takes a turn and the game continues until one side is covered with counters. The first player to cover his side is the winner.

Other games to play

Match-its

Spread out all the word cards face down. Players take turns calling out a word on the page. The word caller then has to find and claim the word by turning over three cards. The player with most cards wins.

Miming game

This game just uses the cards and needs at least three players. Place the cards face up. A player mimes one of the actions. The others try to be the first to pick the right word card to fit the action.

21

Eggs on a plate

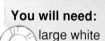
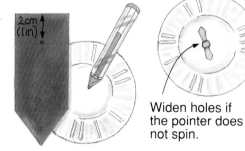

To make the spinner

Turn over a large paper plate and divide it into six sections. Write "egg on" and "egg off" in alternate spaces around the rim.

Cut a piece of thin cardboard 10cm by 2cm (4in by 1in) and trim one end to a point. Paint it red and let it dry.

Use a ballpoint pen to poke a hole in the middle of the plate. Poke another hole in the pointer 1cm (½in) from its straight edge.

Widen holes if the pointer does not spin.

Push a paper fastener through the pointer and the middle of the plate and then open its wings. Make sure the pointer spins smoothly.

To make the eggs

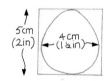

Cut a piece of thin cardboard 4cm by 5cm (1½in by 2in). Draw an egg shape and cut it out. Make 12 of these and decorate them like Easter eggs.

Hints

• Draw and cut out one egg and use the shape to draw the others.

• Instead of decorating the eggs, you could cut six from white paper and six from brown.

To play the game

This is a game for two players. Each player chooses one of the plates on the page.

Players have six eggs each. Before starting, they put three eggs on their plate and leave three off. Both players take turns closing their eyes and moving the pointer with a finger. An egg is moved on or off their plates according to where the pointer stops. The game ends when there are six eggs on a plate, or a plate becomes empty. The player with the most eggs wins. You can shorten the game by setting a time limit, or reducing the number of eggs needed to win.

Other ideas

You can develop this game by changing the words and playing with real objects.

Use toy animals and a chair for "up" and "down". For "back" and "front" turn the toys around.

Put spoons in and out of a cup for "in" and "out".

out in

Alphabet wall hanging

You will need:

 roll of old wallpaper 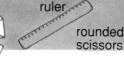 small envelopes ruler rounded scissors pencil paints

To make the wall hanging

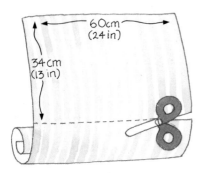

Cut a piece of wallpaper 34cm (13in) by 60cm (24in). This is the backing panel for the wall hanging.

Fold back the flap of a small envelope. Place the envelope so it is close to the long edge of the wallpaper.

Learning notes

This wall hanging will help to make your child familiar with the letters of the alphabet. Once your child learns to recognize letters and know the sounds they represent, he will have a valuable key to reading.

Don't be in a hurry to teach alphabetical order, although you may be surprised at how quickly children learn it, especially if it is sung.

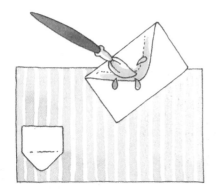

Wet the glued strip on the envelope's flap and stick it onto the wallpaper as shown.

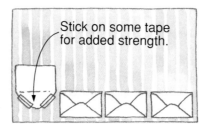

Stick on some tape for added strength.

Fold the envelope back down over its flap. Stick on three more in the same way.

To make the letters

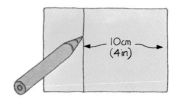

10cm (4in)

Cut four rectangles of wallpaper, 15cm by 10cm (6in by 4in). Draw a line on each piece 10cm (4in) from the short edge.

Turn the paper upside down to draw letters with tails.

In pencil, draw a letter in the space under your drawn line.

Treasure hunt

Scatter pictures around the house. The first player to place three pictures in the correct envelopes is the winner.

If there is only one player see how many pictures can be found to place in the right envelopes.

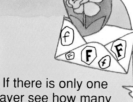

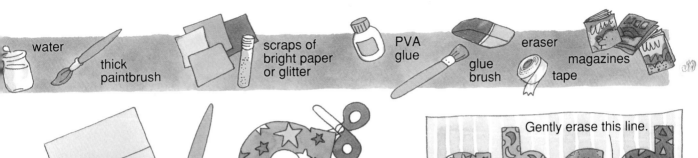

water · thick paintbrush · scraps of bright paper or glitter · PVA glue · glue brush · eraser · magazines · tape

You don't have to cut out the middles.

Gently erase this line.

Paint over the pencil letter with a thick paintbrush. Let the paint dry.

Now cut around the letters and then decorate them by gluing on small pieces of bright paper and glitter. Let the glue dry.

Draw a pencil line on the wallpaper 7cm (3in) from the top of the envelopes. Then glue on the letters, using the line as a guide.

Place the wall hanging within easy reach.

You can cut out lots of letters from magazines and glue them onto the envelopes. You can stick on capital letters as well.

Collect pictures from catalogues or magazines to put into the envelopes. A picture of a cat is put into the "c" envelope and so on.

As your child's knowledge grows you can make more wall hangings, continuing until you have completed the whole alphabet. For older children make a different wall hanging with capital letters.

25

I went to the circus

boots

ball

cup

horse

hat

To play the game

This is a game for two players, although if you have counters in more than two colours you can include other players.

The first player takes a letter out of the bag and says "I went to the circus and I saw..", then tries to find something in the picture beginning with that letter. The labels on the page can be used as a guide. There are plenty of things to spot here: from simple names such as "dog" to more complicated doing words such as "galloping". When something is found, the player then puts her colour counter in the cup. The letters are returned to the bag. The game ends after an agreed time, say, ten minutes. The winner has the most counters in the cup.

26

swinging

shoes

water

pie

balloon

feet

drum

wag

Candy jar

You will need: scraps of bright paper or foil   rounded scissors   black felt-tip pen

To make the counters

Cut 12 candy shapes, as shown, out of scraps of paper or foil. These are your counters.

To make the cards

Make a small mark below letters to show the right way up.

Cut 22 white cards 3cm by 3cm (1½in by 1½in). On each of 21 cards write a letter of the alphabet, leaving out the vowels. Draw a candy cane on the remaining card. This is your joker.

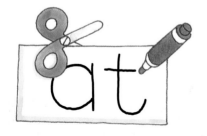

Cut a large card 8cm by 3cm (3in by 1½in). Write the letters "at".

To play the game

This is a game for two players. Before starting, each player chooses one of the candy jars on the page.

Place the card which reads "at" face up. The smaller cards are dealt out, face down, between the players. Players take turns in picking up and placing one of their cards in front of the "at" card to try and make a word. If a player makes a word she can place a counter in her jar. The joker card, when turned up, can stand for any letter. The game ends when all the letters are used. The candies are then added up.

28

thin white cardboard

ruler

Learning notes

This game will help your child recognize that the same groups of letters can occur again and again in making up different words. Tackling groups of letters does not have to be a big step for your child even though she will be learning to link vowel sounds with consonants. Sound the letter and the word endings clearly and then let your child try to join them together. A lot of patience will be needed at first, especially as there are no pictures to help. Remember to explain the meanings of words she may not know.

c at

Hints

● You could collect shiny chocolate wrappers and play this game with real jars. If you don't want to make the counters use buttons or plastic counters.

● To shorten the game you could agree that the first player who puts six candies in the jar is the winner.

Silly sentences

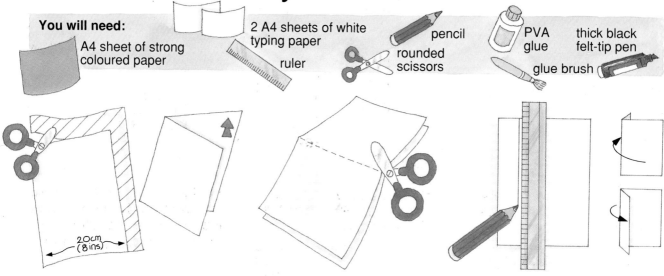

Trim both pieces of white paper so that they measure 28cm by 20cm (11in by 8in). Then fold them so that the short edges meet.

Open the folded sheets and then cut along the middle creases so that you have four separate pieces.

Draw a line on each piece 2cm (1in) from the left-hand long edge. Fold the paper back and then forward along these lines.

Learning notes

This is a fun way to introduce your child to recognizing whole sentences. This is not necessarily a huge step from dealing with individual letters and words, especially if you include words in the flip book with which your child is already familiar.

Other ideas

You can make up sentences about your family and friends, such as "Dad snores in bed" or "Anna walks to school".

Try changing the sentences in your book by gluing a fresh piece of paper on top of the old word strips.

you wash your car

I brush my cat

We wear our hats

they ice their cakes

Draw lines down the pages, leaving a 4cm (2in) gap between each line. You should have four spaces.

Then write a sentence along each page with a thick felt-tip pen.

30

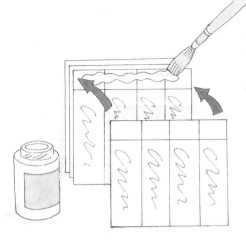

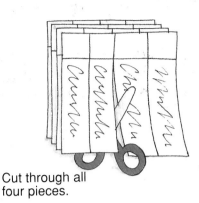

Cut through all
four pieces.

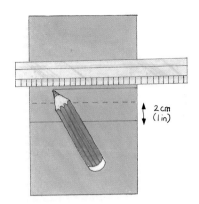

2 cm
(1 in)

Spread a little glue on the
margin of one of the pages
and then press another page
on top. Repeat this until all
the pages are stuck together.

When the glue is dry, cut
along your four drawn lines
to the margin.

Fold your coloured paper so
the short edges meet. Open
it and draw a line 2cm (1in)
from the fold on either side.

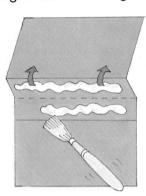

Fold the top page back along
the drawn line to make a
crease. Open it again and
spread glue between the
drawn lines.

we wash your cakes

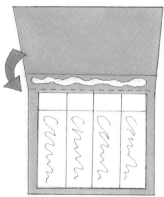

Place the book along the
middle crease. Then close
the cover and press hard
along the glued area.
Let it dry.

Flip over the sections in
your book to read the silly
sentences.

Hint

Spread the glue thinly to keep
the paper from wrinkling.

Materials and equipment

Many of the games in this book involve making things. This is part of the fun so let your child join in such activities as drawing, cutting out and gluing. Talk about the things you are making but try not to make the games sound too complicated: most children will pick up games as you play them. You might want to make the pieces in one play session and play the game in another. You can cover any cards you make with sticky-backed plastic to protect them. Store them in an envelope for safe-keeping.

The specific things you need for each project are listed at the top of each page. Below is some general advice on materials and equipment.

Paper: It is a good idea to keep a box where odd scraps of paper can be collected. This could include large, used envelopes; thin cardboard cut from cereal boxes and such things as shiny wrappers, coloured foil and cellophane. Save old newspapers as you will need these to spread over your work surface, if you are painting or gluing. Magazines make a good source for cut-out pictures and lettering. Rolls of unused wallpaper are excellent for making cards, counters or book covers.

Felt-tip pens should be non-toxic and washable. Try to have both thick and thin pens. For early readers, lettering in black pen on white paper is very clear and easy to read.

Paints: Remember to buy only water-based paints. Ready-mix paints are sold in large stationery stores and stores selling educational toys. You can also use poster paints for small areas. Mix or thin the paints on old plates, and use old mugs for water as they are less easily knocked over than jars. Thick paintbrushes are easier to handle than thin ones. Don't forget to protect all your working surfaces with newspaper.

Scissors should be rounded. If you use sharp scissors remember to put them away immediately after use. If you have to cut out pictures of objects, draw a simple shape around the item so your child can see where to cut.

Glue: PVA glue (polyvinyl acetate) is white but is clear when dry. It can also be used as a varnish or mixed with paint to act as a thickener. Although it does wash out of clothes, it is best to wear aprons or overalls while using it. Wash your brushes immediately after use. You can buy PVA glue in all large stationery stores and stores selling educational toys. Glue sticks are clean and easy to use and are good for sticking small areas. Do not use solvent based glues.

Adhesive tape: Cut all the pieces you need and stick them on a surface ready to use.

Plastic letters are often magnetic and invaluable for many word games. It is good to have two sets as you can then make words and sentences without running out of often-used letters. Try and get both small letters and capitals if possible, although be careful not to mix them at an early stage as this can confuse young children.

Pipe cleaners are sold in craft shops and educational toy stores and come in a great variety. You can also paint ordinary pipe cleaners.

Paper clips: Brass "wing" paper fasteners can be bought in stationers. It is a good idea to keep flat paper clips linked together and make sure all such small objects are out of the reach of very young children.

Paper bags are much safer than plastic ones. Discourage children from putting any kind of bag on their heads - they may not remember which is safe.